I DREAM OF YOU

a different kind of brutha...

NEÖ

B L A Q N E S S

TRUBU PRESS

A Black Legacy Publishing Company

TrubuPRESS is a subsidiary of the Trubu Media Group whose interests include but are not limited to fiction and non fiction stories from the black experience throughout the American and African Diaspora.

Publisher: TrubuPRESS
Editor: Neo Blaqness
Cover Design: TrubuPRESS
Proofreader: Tamika Coleman

I DREAM OF YOU
Copyright © 2013 Neo Blaqness

To order I DREAM OF YOU
visit http://trubupress.com
or call (872) 22TRUBU.

Booksellers:
Retail discounts are available from TrubuPRESS. Inquires about volume orders can be made via the phone number listed above.

ISBN-13: 978-0615772110
ISBN-10: 0615772110
Published by TrubuPRESS
PRINTED IN THE UNITED STATES

Dedication

*"To all who dare
to seek the oft elusive
dream of love"*

CONTENTS

Never Expect p.11

You Are p.13

I Dream of You p.15

I Wish p.17

Prayer of The Modern Man p.19

Prelude to a Kiss p.21

Night Grooves p.23

Melancholy p.25

Somethin's Broke p.27

R U Alright p.29

iiBooG p.31

Vacancy p.33

I Luv Me Sum U p.37

You Made Me Smile Today p.39

That Day p.41

Missin My Liscious p.45

I Know p.47

It's Late p.49

Adieu p.51

Again p.53

Canvas p.55

Sometimes p.57

Choices   p.59

Sistah Friend   p.61

Judas   p.63

Tumbling   p.65

Hav U Eva   p.67

Note to Self   p.69

Voice Unheard   p.71

A Gud Man   p.73

A Gud Woman   p.75

I Can't   p.77

Not This Time   p.79

Convenient Care   p.81

In My Mind   p.85

Afterglow   p.87

A Rose for Sharon   p.89

With Love   p.91

A Home for Love   p.95

Echoes   p.97

The Woman for Me   p.99

Today   p.101

Between   p.103

While You Were Sleeping   p.105

Epilogue   p.107
***
When a Woman Gets   p.109
Into a Man's Shorts

Introduction

A Different Kind of Brutha

Please allow me to introduce you to my heart. *I Dream of You* is my Anthology of Love. Some poems are about real life experiences. Others were inspired by conversations I have had with friends over things they were going through. Still others just happened to be thoughts that crossed my mind and I decided to write about them.

Writing has always been one of my fondest passions and the joy of being able to share my work with those of you who have become fans over the years has been a dream come true.

Included in this collection are some of your favorites along with some of mine. In today's world where so much seems to have been lost to technology, it is good to know that there remains some of us who have a love for the written word. I hope that this collection of poems brings you as much satisfaction as I had writing them.

~NE:O~

"The glass darkly no longer waits for perfection to come;
only for someone to light up the lens ."

I Dream of You

POETIC EXPRESSIONS

a different kind of brutha...

NEö

BLAQNESS

Poetry

Never Expect

Never expect
Someone to carry you
If you are
Unwilling to walk
Never expect
Someone to hear you
If you are
Unwilling to talk
Never expect
Someone to catch you
If you are
Unwilling to fly
Never expect
Someone to live for you
If you are
Afraid to die
Never Expect
Someone to complete you
If you are
Empty inside
Never expect
Someone to find you
If all you
Do is hide
Never expect
Someone to keep you

If all you
Do is fear
Never expect
Someone to need you
If you speak
But fail to hear
Never expect
Someone to forgive you
If you can't
Let go of guilt
Never expect
Someone to love you
If you can't
Love yourself

You Are

You are
More than just a name on my list
More than just someone I wanna step to
More than a temporary guest
In this online world we escape to
You might be wishing for somebody to love
Or maybe somebody to notice
More than the swagga
Of your hips
Your lips
And all the things that
Matter to the eyes
That disguise all that lies
Between the sheets
Of skin within
That voluptuous soul
That tells the story
To those worthy to behold
The glory
That is
Uniquely
U

I Dream of You

Somewhere in my nights
I dream of you
Tho your face I have not known
Nor the colour of your voice
or the brightness of your smile
But still I see you
in that warm glow that remains
long after the sunset
Rippling waters soothe my ears
in the moonlit night
that brings you forth
with the coming tide
On ocean's glass we lay
pressed between
the stars and eternity
These vessels which
we hold so dear
Intertwined
in the ecstasy
of quickened breath
and hottened blood
and milkened white
which both creates life
and feeds the living
In the day
that is still this night

I dream of you
Dreamer that I am
Making real
the folly of my hopes
and the futility of my faith
Such as it is
At least
as I have been judged
unfit to live this daily life
for lack of ability
or willingness
Neither of which
I am quite sure
To follow things so ancient
Relics of truth
worshipped beyond
the meaning of today
A Heathen
to the god of the flat earth
Scorned
that we should enjoy
Blasphemy
in such a love as this
Condemned
only to dream
in black and white
That your hand
might someday
colour my world

I Wish

I wish I could say
I am perfect for you;
But I am not even perfect for myself
I wish I could be
the one who completes you
But giving you all I have
would leave me empty
I wish I could promise you that
I could never love another
But the love I have to give
is meant to be shared
I wish I could be that knight or hero
that sweeps away all your troubles
But then how would you learn
to help another in need
I wish I could be your king
But your spirit should be
subject to NO man
I wish I could promise you
my undivided attention
But you are not my only passion
I wish I could take away
every pain of you heart
But then what wisdom
would you have to offer
I wish I could give you

the riches of the world;
But then what space would be left
for your soul to search or hunger
I wish that I could live
an eternity in your arms
But then how would I know
the treasure that is each
moment with you
I wish I could make you happy
But happiness is not to be found
it is to be lived
I wish I could say
I could never to live without you
But a strong love stays
because it chooses.
And weak love stays
because it has no place else to go
I wish I could raise your self esteem
But if I did, it would no longer be yours
The desires of the heart
are often self-less
Such is the priceless value of love
But each of our lives would be worthless
If granted the wishes above

Prayer of The Modern Man

I WAS NOT BORN TO BE YOUR KING
NEITHER WERE YOU MADE
TO SERVICE ME
THE CHIVALRY
YOU OFT CLAIM TO SEEK
IS MERELY THE SLAVERY
OF A KINDER MASTER
BUT IT IS NOT FREEDOM
TO BE
WHO YOU ARE
TO LOVE
WHAT YOU ARE
TO ANSWER THE CALL
OF YOUR OWN SPIRIT
TO DANCE TO THE MUSIC
OF YOUR MIND
FOR ME TO LOVE YOU
COMPLETELY
I CANNOT HOLD YOU
TO YOUR GENDER
I MUST EMBRACE YOUR SOUL
EQUAL IN EVERY WAY
TO THAT LOVE
I MUST ALSO RESERVE FOR MYSELF
ENTICE ME, THEREFORE
BY YOUR HEART

SEDUCE ME
WITH YOUR MIND
CARESS ME
BY YOUR SPIRIT
THEN
CONSUMMATE INTERWINED
THE FOREPLAY OF ETERNITY
LAY NOT IN A SINGLE TOUCH
BUT IN EVERY OTHER WAY WE FIND
TO SHOW OURSELVES WORTHY
OF EQUAL TRUST
SO LOVE ME
AS YOU KNOW HOW
AND I WILL GLADLY DO THE SAME
LET TRUTH PREVAIL AS YOUR KING
AND LET US BEAR HIS NAME
TOGETHER
NEITHER MAN NOR MATE
NOR WIFE FOR ME
TO SUBJUGATE
BUT KINDRED SPIRITS BE
FAITHFUL TO TRUTH
ABOVE EACH OTHER
LOVING YET FREE
TO DISCOVER
WHEREVER THIS LIFE LEADS

Prelude to a Kiss

It began
in my mind
by the touch
of your words
Gently breathing
on my skin
Caressing me
with vibes unheard
Written thoughts
from a friend
Succulent tasting
salivating
Lips and finger
licking good
Every morsel
you present
got me thinking
if I should
Go there
to a place so real
OOOO
The way you make
my body feel
Warm and moist
and wet and deep
Those unheard words

of yours can speak
They make me writhe
in my sleep
And with each dawn
I change the sheets
Got me wondering
if I'm still me
When I close my eyes
the things I see
All in the moment
that is this
When my mind ponders
our first kiss

Night Grooves

There's a song
moving through my body
inspired by the rhythm of our love
that sweet extemporaneous groove
we laid down last night
where you set the bass
and I followed in the tempo
striking licks on the lead
of the down beat of each measure
while your gyrating sax
blew a soothing tone of ecstasy
taking the reed of your mouth
I breathed into the instrument
of my pleasure
joining the horn section
with the glide of my trombone
as your trumpets stood erect
awaiting my hands to join
in the harmony
of funk and fusion
palming the drums
as they vibrate
to the waves
of sound
arising
from the sheets

of music
as the solo comes to me
full notes, half notes
quarter notes, eighth notes
intensifying beats
pianissimo to mezzo forte
until the last
strike of the drum
reverberates to the bottom
of the bass
and the last
sound of the sax
echoes
into the night

Melancholy

When happiness fails to find you
When memories turn unkind
When tears start to blind you
With pains from your heart and mind
When life dims the brightness of your smile
When hope seems to fade with each passing mile
When it feels like love has been gone a while
Think of me
For I will always hold you in my heart
Fondly remember in my mind
How you stirred my spirit from the start
Helped my soul again to find
A brand new way to live this life
To rise above the burdens and strife
When I am asked how I made it through
I often say because of you
We do not always understand
The meaning nor the master plan
Of how or why we find each other
To be friends or best of lovers
I can only speak what is my truth
Lessons learned from long lost youth
The same that I once helped you find
Within your once unclouded mind
But now the palette has been cleansed
Faded pictures, unfocused lens

Unclear of where to begin again
Blessed with such a cursed sin
Paint your palette blue and gray
Look out on a summer's day
And I will listen as I know how
Perhaps you'll listen now

Somethin's Broke

Somethin's broke
but it ain't my heart
cuz it's still beatin
and it ain't my spirit
cuz it's still leading
me wherever I need to be
but it rattles my brain
when I walk
it swells up my tongue
when I try to talk
it wells up my eyes
when I blink
ties my stomach in knots
when I lay me to sleep
I thought I could cut it out
but I think its too deep
Somethin's broke
I done looked all over
inside myself
and all up under
my thoughts and feelins
my lies my truths
but all I could find
was this here twine
that used to be
tied to my insides

you know that one
you give to your closest friend
to tie up to their other end
so I pulled it
like I usually do
knowing it always
connected to you
'cept this time
it done turned up loose

R U Alright

Today I got that feelin
you know the one
that used to stop me dead
when I'd call and ask
are you alright
and you'd say
damn baby
you must live in my head
'cuz its scary
how you know
just when to call
I'm not used to a man
who won't let me fall
all over the fears
of my imagination
after years of tears
then settlin for masturbation
gettin more satisfaction
from the fingers
on my hand
than the drama that came
wrapped up in a man
I can see you laughing
reading this now
but are you asking yourself
like I am...how

we ended up
like we are today
after all the things
we had to say
funny how life
turns out this way
but
back to that feelin
that won't go away
I'm not tryin to sweat you
but you know
I can't just forget
everything we been through
so pardon
this one time
my interruption
of your life
cuz my heart
won't be fine
til it knows
you're alright

ii Boo G

In case you ever wondered
do I really still think of you
of course I do
even after all the clouds
and storms we been through
you see I am the kind
who neva minded
gettin soaked in the rain
barefoot
hopping puddles
splashing mud
all up in my face
I guess that's part
of the child
still in me
the one who couldn't afford
designer jeans
I wanted to splash
you needed to keep
your Apple Bottoms clean
we each had our way
of looking at the rain
I saw the water as life
you asked
where the hell was da drain
yeah yeah
I know how much you paid

for them thangs
It seems the only thing
that truly separated us
was stuff
I couldn′t care less
you couldn′t get enough
ultimately
the price we paid
was us
It′s not that I minded
all the finer things
but I felt
we were being blinded
by the memories
of what we never had
I feared becoming
just as bad
as the folks
we used to talk about
back in the day
before we got clout
back in the hood
when your hair was nappy
wearin hand me down shoes
but just as happy as me
when we all
used to dance in the rain
one day
I hope you find
that young girl again

Vacancy

There's a place in my bed
where I hate to sleep
I can't even turn
that way no more
without seeing
you looking back at me
with a light
that the darkness
never could absorb
I done slept
in this room
many a day
long before
you was ever here
but the memories of you
won't go away
cant close my eyes
without seeing you clear
can't turn on my back
without feeling your ride
cant sleep to my left
without rememberin
you from behind
walk into this room at night
and I see your silhouette
I still get aroused

by the scent of your sweat
but I done washed everything
yet there's something
that keeps lingering
I think
it's my love for you
when I look to my left
its not that I just
see you missin
from your side of the bed
its the shadow of your smile
when you rubbed my head
touched the hair on my face
kissed me long deep and wet
inside of me
long before I knew
the feel of inside you
and that just can't be replaced
by a bomb azz body
on a pretty young thang
life ain't about tightness
its about how you hang
I'm tired of the whiteness
tryin to stick to me like glue
there ain't nuthin like
the mocha chocolate thyckness of you
dipped with my cinnamon stick
and ready whip cream
all ova those lips
one drink of you
can make a man cuss

damn baby
Starbucks
ain't got sh-t on us
I don't know
maybe all this
is just in my mind
and the emptiness is something
I have no right to redefine
but I can't bring myself
to hang
the vacancy sign

I Luv Me Sum U

gurl I luv me sum u
cuz u got that smile
my mamma use to have
even when she knew
all the things I didn't
about my dad
it's that keep on keepin on
kinda swagg
to let your babies know
things ain't all that bad
even tho
sometimes its for show
to not steal their childhood back
but sometimes
when I see you
I know those eyes
windows to the worries
behind the disguise
you won't say a word
but then I ask
about the tears
behind the mask
you tell me baby
I got class
even if I don't got
a pot to piss in

I ain't tryin to use you
you're my friend
and I tell you baby
I may be worth
more than
what you got
in your purse
but there is no treasure chest
that could hold
the weight
of your heart of gold
and that is why
I luv me some u
cuz even in your needs
you keep doin for you
and still find ways
to give to others
you kno people wonderin
if we be lovers
cuz whenever you're near
they can see right through
to my heart
it's clear
gurl
I luv me sum u

You Made Me Smile Today

You made me smile today
From a thousand miles away
I saw two lovers
Walking hand in hand
Without a single word to say
Their faces
Told it all
And it reminded me
Of you
And all the things
You do
Despite the tragedy
My life
Always seems to be
Whenever I call
You always answer
And I always know
After hello
Life will be better
Than the moment
Just before
I dialed your number
Cuz you always seem to know
How to chase away
My fears
That single word

Dries every tear
Just knowing
That the sound
Of your voice
Means you are near
In the very special way
That only you
Know how to be
You made me smile today
And I wanted you
To see

That Day

The day I almost lost you
was such an ordinary day
went to work
handled my business
in my usual way
Went for a run
sat down for a bite
and then I got
the call
Things for you
weren't going right
no
not right at all
My heart sank
my body ached
I struggled to
breathe air
All I could think
of is why the hell
you wouldn't let
me be right there
by your side
Why
I cried
is this the way it ends
I begged to live

each moment with you
You wanted to spare
your friend
the agony
that you believed
would be
my last memory
of you
But if you could see
and if you only knew
the beauty of
the timeless gift
of love forever true
you gave to me in ways
that no weather
could beat nor fade
The sunshine of my life
you are the breeze
within the shade
The substance in the hollow
for the empty
you are the fill
When storms take flight
you are the Byrd
and I become
your Will
to live this life
I wanted you
forever by my side
The day
I almost lost you

is the day
I wanted to die
We knew
there was a chance
before all
was said and done
That we would miss the dance
we planned
in front of everyone
But the way
I almost lost you
The way
it happened to be
Was worse
than the price
of dreaming
of that life
of you and me
To know
that you were living
and that you
yet may live
But have no memory
of giving me your heart
Twas once
now gone
and never is
Somthin's broke
the Melancholy
of our starry starry nights
An anthology of questions

ending
asking
R U Alright
Forever passed
in quickened time
you answered
me with love
that lingered
beyond the veil
of memories lost
Tis now
what was
And yet
not quite at all
what we
had planned to be
The day
I almost lost you
still ends the day
that will never be

Missin My Liscious

The swagga of your thickness
the passion of your kisses
that nappy doo
that favored you
oh how I miss
my Liscious
banana nut muffin recipe
I only made so I could see
you smile
the way you looked at me
whenever you'd come home
at least
that's how it felt
each time you'd visit
oh God
I miss my Liscious
looking in your eyes
across the candlelight
each night
that you would
serenade me
humming
with each bite
I made
especially for you
I always finished first
sipping wine

to quench my thirst
while you took your time
I cleaned the dishes
oh baby
I miss my Liscious
now tears upon
my pillow be
the same where
you once
shared with me
those nights
that we used
to dream
of everything this is
for my lips
dare not speak
of this as past
my heart
still seeks its echo
alas
fear not my words
that were my last
we both know
what
this is
each day that comes
and goes
my soul knows well
I miss
my Liscious

I Know

I know
I know
I know baby
I know
listen
okay
shhhh
come here
I know baby
(sigh)
it's ok
I know
but it's me
and I'm here
yes
even after all that
I know baby
because I want to
you know that
I want to
you don't have to ask
and I'm not going anywhere
come here baby
I know
it's ok
just
let it out

It's Late

It's late
and
here we both are
you
staring at my words
you can't sleep
but
somehow
this makes you
feel closer
we don't really
know each other
but
I guess
sometimes you think
I might know you
even better than
you know yourself
but you're not here
to get closer
to me
but closer
to the truth
you see
I don't know you
but in
a lot of ways

through letting you
know me
without hiding
my feelings
my failings
and my flaws
you are learning
to let go
of your fears
it's late
and while the
whole world slumbers
you are
finally free
to be
yourself

Adieu

I tried
to help you understand
how much you mean to me
but I soon learned
the best a man can do
is let you see
in silence now
I took my bow
in quiet
took my leave
of all your doubts
despite the shouts
my heart
did heave at me
knowingly
the risk that somehow
you may misperceive
my absence
for a lack of care
but to live
co-dependently
is just not
me
I cannot chase you
make you feel
the way I feel

or how I see
at best
I can show
my heart to you
and hope
you someday see
I know not
how long I have
before my heart
fails me
and tells my mind
that you are lost
despite my disbelief
the place your presence
claimed within
remains
I joyfully visit
now and then
each time
I leave in pain
your absence
is a wound
I can neither patch
nor wish to fill
it reminds me of
the price of love
be that of good or ill
to have the choice
to love or not
for you
I always will

Again

I have walked
as far
as I can go
I have spoken
every word
that I know
I have broken
every rule
that I've learned
crossed every bridge
for you and burned
them all
so hot
this glass once sand
reflects
the co-dependency
of man
this addiction
that the heart
demands
a fixation to love
beyond what can work
and despite the hurt
we do it
again

Canvas

In my mind
there is
a picture of you
in every detail
made only of light
of every hue
no arms
no face
no legs
just grace
and I delight in its view
each night
you colour the skies
of my dreams
the glistening waters
in rolling streams
the fireflies
that light the plains
glowing embers
of distant flames
in everything
I see you
and yet
the only name
I know that's true
is love

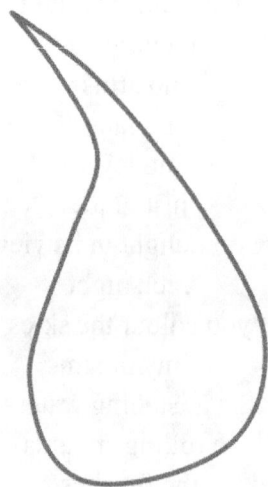

Sometimes

Sometimes
I try
to understand why
Sometimes
I just
start to cry
Sometimes
I wish
I could
hold your hand
Sometimes
just hearing your name
is more
than I can stand
Sometimes
your voice
still lives in my head
Sometimes
your touch
still warms me in bed
Sometimes
I laugh
at things
you once said
Sometimes
I wish

I could still say....
Sometimes
I wish
these memories
would go
away
Sometimes

Choices

There are
many reasons
we let go
Sometimes
our burdens
are too heavy
to expect
another to hold
Or we lack the strength
within our grasp
to find the faith
to simply ask
someone dear
to stand
closer
by our side
focused only
on our pride
Instead
we decide
to hide
Thinking it noble
to fall away
and spare another
the price
you care enough

to pay
Alone
in debt to misery
your heart mortgaged
to a reality
too ashamed
to let anyone see
anymore
And so
close the door
and lock within
all the toxic things
real friends
would take the time
to help you cleanse
It seems the company
you choose to keep
are just the ones
who never sweep
who stir foul mud
and kick up dust
that you inhale
until your lungs
are impaled
and start to wheeze
I can't watch
you suffocate
you have chosen your fate
sometimes it takes
more strength
to leave

Sistah Friend

Holdin on
that was
the easy part
it is
the letting go
that breaks
your heart
that shakes
your faith
in all
that you are
because
you believed
in a love
that didn't last
as long as
you thought
it should
but if you could
go back
to where
it all began
what would
you really
want to
change

strange
that behind
all the pain
are the things
that make us
better
than before
had love
not
knocked
upon your door
had you not
answered
denied
experiencing
more than
the mere chance
of happiness
you would
never know
that you
are blessed
to count it
all joy
no matter the pain
that the testing
of your faith
only makes you
strong enough
to stand
again

Judas

Have you ever been
let down so bad
and so wrong
that only your anger
and frustration
kept you strong
then
later on
when you're calm
you realize
how much harm
was truly done
to your heart
in a flash
go from strong
to falling apart
sometimes we think
the only wounds
are the ones
we got
during the fight
fade to black
next scene
find the knife
that was stuck
in our back

Tumbling

The feeling I had
when I woke up today
I have had
many times before
because that's what
it means to
find someone
you have come
to love
and adore
some might say
that it would hurt
to hear that
you are not
the first
that there have been
others
in the past
may make you believe
that
this won't last
but stop and think
let's be real
it's through heartache
that we learn to feel
and come correct

from past mistakes
we live
we love
we bond
we break
into many pieces
of ourselves
fragile
resting
on the shelf
of life afraid
of the next fall
until we hear
a lover's call
leap our hearts
into a mist
enraptured by
the hidden bliss
we somehow
knew was there
you see faith
is the difference
between
falling in love
or just
tumbling
through the air

Hav U Eva

Have you ever
wanted to believe
so much
that you deceive
your mind
into thinking
you have touched
something
that really
isn't there
Have you ever
hoped
beyond what's real
that you have
made your heart
start to feel
love from someone
who really
does not care
Have you ever
been there
Have you ever
longed so hard
for someone
to hold
that you feel warmth

despite the coldness
of their arms
around you
and yet
despite the truth
you substitute
all you have inside
to make up
for the love denied
from all
the people
in your life
girlfriend
boyfriend
husband
wife
this is
no way to live
but then
you know that
already
how much of you
will you keep
betting
will be left
when you have
nothing else
to give

Note to Self

Woman looks up
from being struck
down by the hands
of her man
through her cries
he asks her
why are you
even here
and she replies
because there is
only one person
who hates me
more than you
then proceeds
to wipe
her tears
in the mirror

Voice Unheard

I never used to
understand why
it was so important when
the day would end
and you'd complain
that you didn't hear my voice
until I had no choice
and could no longer call
now I listen for your presence
to hear no sound at all
just the silence of my heart
alone beating
the echo that was lost
fleeting hopes
that the cost
of my indifference
would not be this
that I should long
to hear from you
the same way now of me
that you once missed

A Gud Man

Wut a good man does
that anutha can't do
is kno how to love u
after the luvin is thru
he don't just roll ova
he still wants next to u
makin luv to ur mind
workin up to round two
thoughts and hearts intertwined
in ways a body can't do
makin u realize
there's a size
inside of him
bigger than wut
was in between yo thighs
that makes every otha brutha
small thru the lense
of luv as u look in his eyes
touching u in ways
that makes another touch lie
and the otha brutha
dont even kno
he has no chance becuz
he can't touch u
in ways
that a good man does

A Gud Woman

Wut a good woman does
that no other can do
is sho you the luv
even when life happens to do
you wrong in ways
sometimes you even deserve
she wraps you in her arms
and says I love you
first
but then she don't leave it there
cuz for a good woman to say
she really cares
will go on to tell you
bout yo self
she ain't tryin to be
yo trophy on no shelf
she wants things to move on
from the way it was
and she will walk with you thru it
cuz thats wut
a good woman does

I Can't

I cant fight the ghosts
of every man
who eva dun you wrong
I can't fill the space
of every place
where you never felt
like you belonged
I cant bear the pain
of every heart
that turned against your own
I cant battle every demon
who has made your life its home
I cant take the blame
for every choice
I was not around to make
or speak for every
nameless voice
who said nothing
while you made mistakes
I cant account
for what you never felt
from the men who kept you warm
and left their seed
inside you while
they went to another's arms
there are many things

I cannot do
I can only look above
and ask my Father
to strengthen you
and fill me with his love
that I might stand
the tempest still
beside you hand in hand
abide me now
within His will
that I might be
your man

Not This Time

There comes a time
when someone must
have the courage
to say
goodbye
and admit to ones self
as much as you tried
tho no one is wrong
something's not right
we can prolong it
find all the reasons
to fight on
pretend that it's all
we hoped it could be
when in reality
its all about
the convenience
of me
and you
only when you feel
the need
when filled to capacity
your heart
prefers to be free
who am I to complain
that's exactly how

I used to be
but now that I'm grown
I understand
the demands
of the heart
needing a home
beyond the measure
of intertwined thighs
and passionate pleasures
true love
needs eyes
to look into
a voice to befriend you
when all around you
the world befalls
love finds that moment
in eternity
to call
if only to say
you were on my mind
someday
you may find it
but I'm afraid
not this time

Convenient Care

There's not a day
that I forgot to say
I love you
not a single day
forget to say
I care
not a day went by
I didn't work
to know your struggles
not a day
that you didn't know
that I was here
not a day that
I put myself above you
not a day
I didn't lift
you up in prayer
not a day
when we met
I didn't hug you
or seek ways
to case your
pain and many fears
but everyday
you asked
for understanding

and when given it
you only asked for more
making me feel as if
I was too demanding
that I should ask
that you should
practice opening doors
that you hid behind
instead of being truthful
with yourself
and someone
that you claim you love
passing notes in class
was cute when we were youthful
but for grown ass
men and women
it's not enough
the silent little woman
of the fifties
might work for
big d-ck men with little brains
but for real men of today
that sh-t feels shifty
now it feels like
all my care
has been in vain
it's not that I believe
you never loved me
or think somehow
you ever meant me harm
but taking me for granted

came too easy
sabotaging simple things
at every turn
I don't know if
it's that you feel unworthy
or maybe somehow feel
deserving of more
I'm content to know
my love was not self serving
and unlike the past
this time content
to close the door
not with malice nor hatred
neither is there sadness
I do this so
my sanity is spared
I can't live another day
within the madness
of my heart
on life support
at convenient care

In My Mind

I spend a lot of time
thinking about you
maybe more than I should
nah not in that way
you think I do
aiight I'm lyin
but gurl
those dreams
are off da hook
still that's not all
I dream about things
I never thought
I'd say out loud
cuz a brutha
gotta play it cool
now I'm sounding
like we back
in high school
but for real
that's how I feel
when I look at you
as old as we are now
I feel brand new
every single day
I'm blessed
to have you near
if only
in my mind

Afterglow

Its been a while now
perhaps even longer on my part
time never moved fast
since you been on my heart
maybe
its because
I never wanted it to
I wanted each second
to last a moment
moments
to last hours
hours
to be a lifetime
that I would never
awake without you
so much so
that I dared not
close my eyes
tho sleep begged me for mercy
I deprived my body
for the sake of my heart
my mind
for the sake of my soul
my life
for the sake of my spirit
never wanting to miss

a single blink of life
the picture looked so perfect
with you in it
how now
can I imagine my sky
without the radiance of your sun
my nights
without the stars in your eyes
my winters
without the warmth
of your heart
my springs
without the flowers
of your blessed place beside me
my summers
without your soothing kisses
my autumns
without the song of you
that rustled through
the falling leaves
for my world no longer turns
now that you are gone
so too have I lost
the seasons of my life
an unceasing winter
kept alive
only by
the lingering embers
of the fire
that was once
you and me

A Rose for Sharon

Before the winters
of our discontent
after the summer
that we met
I made the trek
while you slept
twenty miles
just to uncover
the snow
that piled upon
the windows
of your car
opened the door
to leave a card
and a fistful
of chocolate kisses
on your seat
because you had
no Valentine
I just figured
I would make you mine
but that was many wounds ago
little did I know
how deep the hurt
had already flowed
into the many

crevices of your life
but what I came
to later understand
despite all the
things that happened
is that I was made
to endure
and I prepared
as best I could
for the moment that
I knew you would
eventually cast upon me more
weight than I had
ever known before
but I bore it because
you could bear no more
I am now
what I will always be
what I was meant to be
before you and me
and yet there is more
I've come to see
because of you
there will yet be a time
when we can look back
at that Valentines
without regret
for the paths we chose
for you possess the greatest gifts
the blossoming seeds
from a single rose

With Love

We had a love
for all the wrong reasons
you were looking for
someone to believe in
you for a change
and not just complain
about all of the things
you never could be
instead of the things you are
And so everyday
you awoke with
the painful reminders
of living a lie
to yourself most of all
and then began
quite a fall
while I constantly
called you to fly
Instead you reached out
your hand to me
I questioned your sanity
when you were
trying your best
not to die
I could easily reason then
many things from

the weariness
it brought to my life
what has remained then as now
on my mind is somehow
I should have found a way
despite all the strife
I guess in the end
I was not quite the friend
I always promised to be
but it wasn't revenge
that made me step away
It was that we were
too close to see
through the darkness
and dust we heaped
on each other
clawing and crumbling
our way out to breathe
and now that the air
has found it's way clear
and we have managed to achieve
freedom from that prison
we can finally listen
to what our hearts
must have known all along
that if given fair chance
the notes of romance
would have eventually
written our song
Instead we were soldiers
battling composers

marching to different beats
it seems that the only
harmony we shared
was written between the sheets
I admit I didn't cry
the day the music died
for so long
it became just a noise
Sounding brass
tinkling symbols
of love in a thimble
we both knew well deserved
to be more
Now in the silence of years
I have found all the tears
you deserved from me
well before
our time got away
still there's time yet to say
Come what may
there will never be enough
memories of pain
that the enemy can bring
to stop me from thinking
of you
only
With Love

Home is where the heart is...

A Home for Love

looking sexy might catch an eye
but being humble will catch a heart
a compliment might stroke an ego
but does your presence stir a soul
when you say something
you speak to a mind
when you are quiet
a spirit listens
the one who wants you
for only what you show
is too unwise to know
that the best of you
remains unseen
covered by the vanity
of your insecurity
it is the morning you
that tells the truth
when the rising sun
outshines the moon
you will have made
a home for love

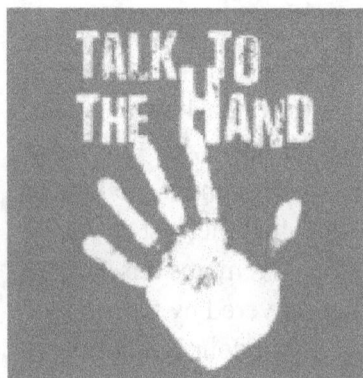

Echoes

I heard you
the other day
I swear
it was only in my head
but I heard
my mouth say
things that used to
make me scream
inside when you
used to say
them to me
and I'd roll my eyes
say "talk to the hand"
cuz you must think
I'm three
I'm a grown ass woman
believe me
I showed you
last night
between those sheets
then you would
walk away
in silence
while my mind
went violent
thinking

you laughing at me
no wonder you
hit the streets
cuz looking back at that
I wouldn't want
to live with me
but it's crazy
how things linger
sittin with my niece
waggin my finger
thinkin I'm givin
her a piece
of my mind
when part of it
is yours
I just wanted
you to know
you left some things
when you went
out the door
too big for me
to wear before
but I grew
into them well
yes we had
our nights
of heaven
but still
I want to say
sorry
for the hell

The Woman for Me

I have never been into the wifey types
a woman who just gives up her life
to a man and bonds herself
to his every wish
as though she exists
for his every command
I always thought
there's got to be
something better than this
that a woman should bow
for lack of a d-ck
and yet it seems
every woman I meet
from the day she was made
has been taught to be a slave
to humble herself at a mans feet
sorry but that not a woman
at least not a woman for me
I glory most
in an undependent mind
more than the junk in the trunk
of a healthy behind
that wiggles and jiggles
to service me
just so I allow my wallet
to be empty

wow, legalized prostitution
that's quite a marriage vow
but there are those yet still
who will call it love
somehow ordained
by some nameless god above
if that be what your faith
calls you to do
who am I to question
what works for you
as for me and my house
we will serve each other
not lion and mouse
but EQUAL and together
in all things
not by the rules of some book
pieced together
by pale faced crooks
who stole lands
and gained fame
for things he never discovered
then raped our mothers
in Jesus name
a woman for me
be she ghetto and loud
Lakisha Shanita
Afrocentric and proud
is everything
I will ever need
she don't have to be perfect
as long as she is free

Today

Today
when you looked at me
your eyes smiled with the innocence
of a girl who had never known sadness
Your face glowed
like a child given a long awaited gift
You tilted your head and blushed
like a teenager
whose first love admitted
to feeling the same way about you
And yet the years between
those days and today
have been long
with every reason
for that innocence to be lost
and face lined with disappointment
and heart hardened by battle
But somehow
the love that is there
when we share a glance
covers the multitude of sins
between your heart and mine
with a bed of the Rose of Sharon
and a fragrance of that sweet spirit
which pollinates through the winds of time
the path which is our future
Would that I walk

and not trample upon this seed
nor crush a single petal
of so blossoming a love as this
that the flower of my new day
might bloom forever

Between

In the silence
between each breath
I speak your name
between each blink
I see your face
when my lips part
I feel your kiss
between each second
It's you I miss
between each beat
my heart does pause
to hear its echo
in the rhythm of yours
between the distance
of earth and sky above
in the instant of now
it is you
that I love

While You Were Sleeping

Before the dawn
of each day
when your face
is at rest
I gaze upon
my love
looking her best
no makeup
no glamour
no rush to impress
at peace in the skin
God made you in
perfection
at last
til you open your eyes
surprised by my stare
your mind starts to cry
"Oh my God my hair"
then you see me smile
and your heart understands
that while you were sleeping
I became
your man

Epilogue

If you died today
and the only thing
that mattered
for your soul
to be saved
is that you truly
loved someone
what could you say
that you
once gave your heart
but did you
give your all
did you
play it safe
did you leap
or did you fall
were you terrified
or did you
enjoy the ride
despite knowing
it could end
you see
the secret of life
is not how love can't fail
but that it always
can begin

a different kind of brutha...

NEö
BLAQNESS

Bonus Essay

When a Woman Gets
Into a Man's Shorts

Today I finally had the courage to open that drawer. The one I set aside for her to use whenever she would visit. Where she would leave the things that made it feel like home- knowing that each time she came back seeing it just the way she left it, that a part of her lived here even when she was gone.

Her bath sponge still hangs next to mine. Her shampoo and conditioner rest in the bathroom cabinet with the extra contact lens case we stopped past the dollar store to get one time when she was here.

Food I bought only because I knew she liked it-the little comforts that spoke to others that she had been here and; obviously, loved by me.

In the past when we would have our differences and think that it was all over, I never could put those things away. To throw them in the trash was like a sin against my own heart. So they would remain as a solemn reminder of my stubbornness or her stupidity or vice versa.

I would shower and she would be there. I would shave and she would be there. Go to the kitchen and she would be there… until the food spoiled so rotten that I had no choice but to throw it out. I could never eat it. It was meant for my hands to prepare it for her.

The sofa where we shared our first kiss, my bed where we first made love, the pillows where we rested for hours looking into each others eyes and just talking; that mirror that reflected our passions that day when we both happened to look up at the same time from the sweat pouring over our bodies. Oh how I wish sometimes I could just replace it all.

But somehow, in spite of the memories that haunt my every turn, I could never quite get myself to open that drawer, until today. You see, I had always been so organized before she went away. Everything folded and in the right place. Since she's been gone, it's all been as dusty and tossed about as our love.

This all came about because I did my laundry. Having organized every drawer I could not find the bottom half to one of my gym sets. I looked all over, under the bed, back in the laundry room, cleared out the closet knowing full well where they were but still having to prove it in my mind- to give myself a reason to open that drawer.

The reality is, I never wore those shorts again since the day she borrowed them. I washed them and I put them back. And each time she would wear them and put them in with my laundry they always went back into her drawer.

And so, after a deep breath, I opened the drawer. The extra set of combs for her hair, the simple tank top she looked so sexy in running to the bathroom, and, yes, my shorts. Out of all the things on which her memory lingers, this was the most emotional reminder of her… because life changes when a woman gets into a man's shorts.

There are so many signs of who a woman is and wishes to be in your life. Like if she even comes over to your house, then she is ready to know the real you. If she lets you cook for her, she has confidence in your judgment. If she takes off her shoes and curls up on your couch, your grooming impresses her. If she kisses you, your presence attracts her. If she looks in your eyes to talk to you, your spirit reaches her. If she takes off her wig or extensions (I'm just sayin…lol) she wants you to know the real her. If she lays in your arms after the loving, it is where she truly hopes to be for the rest of her life.

Now all of that may seem like a lot. And, indeed, it means a lot and says a lot about true romance between people. But when a woman gets into a man's shorts, it is a message that is deeper than sex. A man's shorts is where he sweats his balls off. A man's shorts is where he might start to leak if a woman has made him horny. A man's shorts tells everything about a man's hygiene.

For a woman to get up from sex and put her bare coochie in a man's shorts is more powerful than her swallowing a nut. Because even if the man has good hygiene, she still has to trust that he knows how to do laundry. There is a reason most women wash their panties by hand. They don't want any heavy detergent irritating things down there. But most men don't give that a single thought when they put half the soap box in a single load. So when a woman gets into a man's shorts it is as close to putting a ring on a finger that she can get.

I never realized until today what it meant to me the day she asked to borrow them and I reached over and pulled them out of my drawer and gave them to her. How much it changed me to see her in something that was a reflection of my manhood that she wore in such a new and sexy way. They would never be mine again.

I remember wanting to wear that color short set to match up with the guys I was playing football with and I went mismatched because they weren't mine anymore; and I couldn't just replace them with a duplicate set. I simply said I lost them. Well, it was a half truth- I did lose them... to her.

And I was thinking today that there are so many ways a woman gets into a man's mind and into his heart.

But when a woman gets into a man's shorts, he sees a vision of himself and everything he hopes to have in his life.

When a woman gets into a man's shorts, he learns that the body may be strong but the heart is fragile and needs care.

When a woman gets into a man's shorts, he understands that it takes more than d-ck to wear the pants and that there is value to the substance of who she is.

When a woman gets into a man's shorts, she validates her acceptance of his manhood and he confirms her place equal in his heart.

When a woman gets into a man's shorts, she adds to his glory the compassion of her wisdom reminding him that might and power alone is not the measure of greatness.

When a woman gets into a man's shorts, it is the ultimate symbol of one-ness; that she is standing where he stands.

Someday, I will have to take down her bath sponge. I will have to throw out her shampoo and the conditioner. But today, I had to, simply, close that drawer. I can't say I truly understand myself what it all means, but to empty it is not an option. Because, for now, that is where my love lives.